The Chicken Soup Cookbook

50 Delicious Chicken Soup Recipes to Warm Your Heart

By
BookSumo Press

Published by
http://www.booksumo.com

LEGAL NOTES

Table of Contents

Western European Style Chicken Soup 26

Nutty Potato Chicken Soup 27

Japanese Inspired Bamboo and Mushroom Chicken Soup 28

Arizona Inspired Chicken Soup 29

Pennsylvanian Dutch Style Chicken Soup with Rivels 30

Ramen Noodle Chicken Soup 31

Late September's Best Chicken Soup 32

Full-Ingredient Chicken Soup 33

Thursday Night Dinner Chicken Soup 34

Alternative Asian Chicken Soup 36

Manhattan Island Chicken Soup 37

Chicken Soup Sampler 38

Chicken Soup with Garden Salsa 39

6-Ingredient Creamy Chicken Soup 40

Chicken Soup Dublin Inspired 41

60-Minute Chicken Soup 42

Grocery Rotisserie Orzo Chicken Soup 43

30-Minute Mediterranean Chicken Soup 44

Upstate NY Inspired Chicken Soup 45

I ♥ Chicken Soup 46

Tuesday's Spicy Chicken Ramen Noodle Soup 47

Southwest
Chicken Soup

🥣 Prep Time: 10 mins
🕐 Total Time: 50 mins

Servings per Recipe: 4
Calories	486 kcal
Fat	19.8 g
Carbohydrates	55.2g
Protein	25.2 g
Cholesterol	51 mg
Sodium	1618 mg

Ingredients

2 skinless, boneless chicken breasts cut into cubes
1/2 tsp olive oil
1/2 tsp minced garlic
1/4 tsp ground cumin
2 (14.5 oz.) cans chicken broth
1 C. frozen corn kernels

1 C. chopped onion
1/2 tsp chili powder
1 tbsp lemon juice
1 C. chunky salsa
8 oz. corn tortilla chips
1/2 C. shredded Monterey Jack cheese

Directions

1. In a large pan, heat oil on medium heat and sear the chicken for about 5 minutes.
2. Stir in the garlic, cumin, broth, corn, onion, chili powder, lemon juice and salsa.
3. Reduce the heat to low and simmer for about 20 - 30 minutes.
4. Break up some tortilla chips into serving bowls and top with the hot soup.
5. Serve with a topping of the Monterey Jack cheese and a little sour cream.

CHICKEN
Soup 101

Prep Time: 10 mins
Total Time: 25 mins

Servings per Recipe: 4
Calories	150 kcal
Fat	4.6 g
Carbohydrates	10.8g
Protein	17.1 g
Cholesterol	41 mg
Sodium	289 mg

Ingredients

1 boneless chicken breast half, cooked
and diced
2 C. water
2 carrots, chopped
1 zucchini, diced
1 clove garlic, minced

1/2 tsp chicken broth base

Directions

1. In a large pan, add cooked chicken meat and water and bring to a boil.
2. Add the carrots, zucchini and garlic and simmer for about 5-10 minutes.
3. Add the chicken broth and simmer for an about 5 minutes.
4. Serve hot.

Chicken Soup
Spicy Mexican Style

Prep Time: 20 mins
Total Time: 40 mins

Servings per Recipe: 8
Calories	377 kcal
Fat	19.1 g
Carbohydrates	30.9g
Protein	23.1 g
Cholesterol	46 mg
Sodium	943 mg

Ingredients

1 onion, chopped
3 cloves garlic, minced
1 tbsp olive oil
2 tsp chili powder
1 tsp dried oregano
1 (28 oz.) can crushed tomatoes
1 (10.5 oz.) can condensed chicken broth
1 1/4 C. water
1 C. whole corn kernels, cooked
1 C. white hominy

1 (4 oz.) can chopped green chili peppers
1 (15 oz.) can black beans, rinsed and drained
1/4 C. chopped fresh cilantro
2 boneless chicken breast halves, cooked and cut into bite-sized pieces
Crushed tortilla chips
Sliced avocado
Shredded Monterey Jack cheese
Chopped green onions

Directions

1. In a large pan, heat the oil on medium heat and sauté the onion and garlic till soft.
2. Stir in the chili powder, oregano, tomatoes, broth and water and bring to a boil.
3. Simmer for about 5-10 minutes.
4. Stir in the corn, hominy, chilis, beans, cilantro, and chicken and simmer for about 10 minutes.
5. Transfer the soup into serving bowls and serve with a topping of the crushed tortilla chips, avocado slices, cheese and chopped green onion.

CLASSICAL
Southern Italiana Chicken Soup

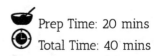

Prep Time: 20 mins
Total Time: 40 mins

Servings per Recipe: 6

Calories	398 kcal
Fat	20.1 g
Carbohydrates	23.9g
Protein	29.8 g
Cholesterol	112 mg
Sodium	839 mg

Ingredients

1 tbsp olive oil
1 small onion, diced
3 stalks celery, diced
3 cloves garlic, minced
2 carrots, shredded
1 lb. cooked, cubed chicken breast
4 C. chicken broth
1 (16 oz.) package mini potato gnocchi
1 (6 oz.) bag baby spinach leaves

1 tbsp cornstarch
2 tbsp cold water
2 C. half-and-half cream
Salt and ground black pepper to taste

Directions

1. In a large pan, heat the oil on medium heat and sauté the onion, celery, garlic and carrots for about 5 minutes.
2. Stir in the cubed chicken and chicken broth and bring to a gentle boil.
3. Stir in the gnocchi and cook for about 3-4 minutes.
4. Stir in the spinach and simmer for about 3 minutes.
5. Meanwhile in a small bowl, dissolve the cornstarch in the cold water.
6. Add the cornstarch mixture and half-and-half in the simmering soup and stir to combine.
7. Simmer for about 5 minutes.
8. Stir in the salt and black pepper and serve.

Zuppa Pollo

Prep Time: 20 mins
Total Time: 40 mins

Servings per Recipe: 10
Calories	227 kcal
Fat	8.1 g
Carbohydrates	18.2g
Protein	19.2 g
Cholesterol	74 mg
Sodium	1124 mg

Ingredients

4 C. chopped, cooked chicken meat
1 C. chopped celery
1/4 C. chopped carrots
1/4 C. chopped onion
1/4 C. butter
8 oz. egg noodles
12 C. water

9 cubes chicken bouillon
1/2 tsp dried marjoram
1/2 tsp ground black pepper
1 bay leaf
1 tbsp dried parsley

Directions

1. In a large pan, melt the butter and sauté the celery and onion till tender.
2. Add the chicken, carrots, water, bouillon cubes, marjoram, black pepper, bay leaf and parsley and simmer for about 30 minutes.
3. Add the noodles and simmer for about 10 minutes.

CHICKEN SOUP
Base 101

Prep Time: 20 mins
Total Time: 1 hr 15 mins

Servings per Recipe: 8
Calories	338 kcal
Fat	21.3 g
Carbohydrates	5.8g
Protein	29.5 g
Cholesterol	91 mg
Sodium	118 mg

Ingredients

2 quarts chicken broth
1 quart water
1 store-bought roast chicken
3 tbsp vegetable oil
2 large onions cut into medium dice
2 large carrots, peeled and cut into
rounds or half rounds, depending on
size

2 large stalks celery, sliced 1/4 inch thick
1 tsp dried thyme leaves

Directions

1. In a large pan, add the broth and water on medium-high heat and bring to a boil.
2. Meanwhile, separate the chicken meat from the skin and bones and reserve in a bowl.
3. Add the skin and bones in the simmering broth and stir to combine.
4. Reduce the heat to low and simmer, covered partially for about 20-30 minutes.
5. Through a colander, strain the broth in a large container.
6. Reserve the broth and discard the skin and bones.
7. In the same pan, heat the oil on medium-high heat and sauté the onions, carrots and celery for about 8-10 minutes.
8. Add the chicken, broth and thyme and bring to a boil.

Fired Roasted Chicken Soup with Black Beans

🥣 Prep Time: 20 mins
🕐 Total Time: 1 hr 15 mins

Servings per Recipe: 10
Calories	143 kcal
Fat	5.5 g
Carbohydrates	15.6g
Protein	12.4 g
Cholesterol	24 mg
Sodium	714 mg

Ingredients

2 tbsp vegetable oil
1 lb. skinless, boneless chicken breasts cut into strips
1 (1.27 oz.) packet fajita seasoning
1 red bell pepper, cut into thin strips
1 green bell pepper, cut into thin strips
1 Poblano pepper, cut into thin strips

1 large onion, cut into thin strips
1 (14.5 oz.) can fire roasted diced tomatoes
1 (15 oz.) can seasoned black beans
1 (14 oz.) can chicken broth
1 dash hot sauce
Salt and pepper to taste

Directions

1. In a large pan, heat the oil on medium heat and cook the chicken for about 10 minutes, stirring occasionally.
2. Add the fajita seasoning and stir till well combined.
3. Add the bell peppers, Poblano pepper and onion on medium heat and cook for about 10 minutes.
4. Add the fire roasted tomatoes, black beans and chicken broth and bring to a boil on high heat.
5. Reduce the heat to medium-low and simmer, uncovered for about 30 minutes, stirring occasionally.
6. Stir in the hot sauce, salt and pepper and serve immediately.

CHEDDAR
and Broccoli Chicken Soup

 Prep Time: 10 mins

Total Time: 1 hr 10 mins

Servings per Recipe: 10

Calories	434 kcal
Fat	26.6 g
Carbohydrates	15.3g
Protein	33.4 g
Cholesterol	129 mg
Sodium	1059 mg

Ingredients

1/2 C. butter
1 C. all-purpose flour
11 C. water
3 cubes chicken bouillon
2 lb. skinless, boneless chicken breast
halves - cut into bite-size pieces
2 heads fresh broccoli, cut into florets
1 1/2 tsp salt

1 tsp ground black pepper
1 C. light cream
3 C. shredded Cheddar cheese

Directions

1. In a large pan, melt the butter on medium heat and cook the flour till a thick paste forms, stirring continuously.
2. Transfer the paste into a bowl and keep aside.
3. In the same pan, add the water, bouillon cubes, chicken, broccoli, salt and pepper on high heat and bring to a boil.
4. Reduce the heat to medium-low and simmer for about 45 minutes.
5. Slowly, add the flour paste, stirring continuously.
6. Simmer for about 5 minutes.
7. Reduce heat and stir in the cream.
8. Slowly, add the cheese, 1 C. at a time and stir till melts completely.

Hearty Chili
Chicken Soup

🥣 Prep Time: 15 mins
🕐 Total Time: 1 hr 10 mins

Servings per Recipe: 6
Calories	418 kcal
Fat	22.3 g
Carbohydrates	24.4g
Protein	29.2 g
Cholesterol	69 mg
Sodium	796 mg

Ingredients

6 tbsp vegetable oil
8 (6 inch) corn tortillas, coarsely chopped
6 cloves garlic, minced
1/2 C. chopped fresh cilantro
1 onion, chopped
1 (29 oz.) can diced tomatoes
2 tbsp ground cumin

1 tbsp chili powder
3 bay leaves
6 C. chicken broth
1 tsp salt
1/2 tsp ground cayenne pepper
5 boneless chicken breast halves, cooked

Directions

1. In a large pan, heat the oil and sauté the tortillas, garlic, cilantro and onion for about 2-3 minutes.
2. Stir in the tomatoes and bring to a boil.
3. Stir in the cumin, chili powder, bay leaves, salt, cayenne and chicken stock and again bring to a boil.
4. Reduce the heat to medium and simmer for about 30 minutes.
5. Discard the bay leaves and stir in the chicken and cook till heated completely.
6. Serve hot.

CHICKEN SOUP
with Avocado

🥣 Prep Time: 20 mins
🕐 Total Time: 1 hr 40 mins

Servings per Recipe: 6	
Calories	315 kcal
Fat	16.4 g
Carbohydrates	12.1g
Protein	29.2 g
Cholesterol	80 mg
Sodium	1368 mg

Ingredients

1 1/4 lb. skinless, boneless chicken
breast halves
2 tbsp taco seasoning mix
1 tbsp vegetable oil
1/2 C. chopped onions
1/2 C. chopped celery
2 tsp ground cumin
1/4 tsp ground black pepper
1 C. water

3 (14 oz.) cans chicken broth
1 C. diced tomatoes
1 tbsp chopped fresh cilantro
1 C. shredded Cheddar cheese
1 C. crushed tortilla chips
1 avocado - peeled, pitted and diced

Directions

1. Set your oven to 350 degrees F before doing anything else.
2. Arrange the chicken breasts onto a baking sheet and sprinkle with 1 tbsp of the taco seasoning mix evenly.
3. Cook in the oven for about 30 - 35 minutes.
4. Remove the chicken breasts from the heat and keep aside to cool.
5. Cut the chicken breasts into strips.
6. Meanwhile in a large pan, heat the oil and sauté the onions and celery till soft.
7. Stir in the water, chicken broth, cumin, black pepper and remaining taco seasoning mix and simmer for about 30 minutes.
8. Stir in the tomatoes, cilantro and chicken and simmer for about 5 minutes.
9. Serve hot with a topping of the avocado, shredded cheese and crushed tortilla chips.

Tuesday's
Chicken Soup Orzo

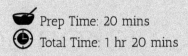 Prep Time: 20 mins

Total Time: 1 hr 20 mins

Servings per Recipe: 12

Calories	167 kcal
Fat	4.1 g
Carbohydrates	21.7g
Protein	12.1 g
Cholesterol	20 mg
Sodium	187 mg

Ingredients

8 oz. orzo pasta
1 tsp olive oil
3 carrots, chopped
3 ribs celery, chopped
1 onion, chopped
2 cloves garlic, minced
1/2 tsp dried thyme
1/2 tsp dried oregano
Salt and ground black pepper to taste
1 bay leaf

3 (32 oz.) cartons fat-free, low-sodium chicken broth
1/2 C. fresh lemon juice
1 lemon, zested
8 oz. cooked chicken breast, chopped
1 (8 oz.) package baby spinach leaves
1 lemon, sliced for garnish
1/4 C. grated Parmesan cheese

Directions

1. In a large pan of lightly salted boiling water, cook the orzo for about 5 minutes.
2. Drain well and rinse under cold water to cool completely.
3. In a large pan, heat the olive oil on medium heat and cook the carrots, celery and onion for about 5-7 minutes.
4. Add the garlic and sauté for about 1 minute.
5. Stir in the thyme, oregano, salt, black pepper and bay leaf and sauté for about 30 seconds.
6. Add the chicken and bring to a boil.
7. Reduce the heat to medium-low and simmer, covered partially for about 10 minutes.
8. Stir in the orzo, lemon juice, lemon zest and chicken and simmer for about 5 minutes.
9. Stir in the baby spinach and simmer for about 2-3 minutes.
10. Serve hot with a garnishing of the lemon slices and Parmesan cheese.

VEGGIE GNOCCHI
Chicken Soup

Prep Time: 20 mins
Total Time: 45 mins

Servings per Recipe: 8
Calories	311 kcal
Fat	20.6 g
Carbohydrates	19.7g
Protein	11.7 g
Cholesterol	43 mg
Sodium	854 mg

Ingredients

1/2 C. margarine
3/4 C. finely chopped onion
3/4 C. finely chopped celery
1/2 C. finely grated carrot
1 1/2 tsp minced garlic
1/3 C. all-purpose flour
4 C. chicken broth
3/4 C. half-and-half
3/4 C. milk

1 (16 oz.) package potato gnocchi
1 1/2 C. chopped cooked chicken
3/4 C. shredded fresh spinach
1/2 tsp dried rosemary
1/2 tsp salt
1/4 tsp ground black pepper
1/4 tsp nutmeg

Directions

1. In a large pan, melt the butter on medium heat and cook the onion, celery, carrot and garlic for about 5-10 minutes.
2. Stir in the flour and cook for about 3-4 minutes, stirring continuously.
3. Stir in the chicken broth, half-and-half and milk and bring to a boil.
4. Boil for about 5 minutes.
5. Reduce the heat to low and stir in the gnocchi, chicken, spinach, rosemary, salt, black pepper and nutmeg.
6. Simmer for about 8-10 minutes.

Cream
of Chicken Soup

Prep Time: 15 mins
Total Time: 35 mins

Servings per Recipe: 8
Calories	852 kcal
Fat	48.9 g
Carbohydrates	65.7g
Protein	41.3 g
Cholesterol	139 mg
Sodium	2166 mg

Ingredients

3 cloves garlic, minced
1 onion, chopped
3 tbsp margarine
2 tbsp all-purpose flour
3 (14 oz.) cans chicken broth
4 C. half-and-half
1 (10.75 oz.) can condensed cream of chicken soup
1 C. fresh salsa
1 (15 oz.) can creamed corn

6 skinned, boneless, chicken breast halves, cooked
2 tsp ground cumin
1 (1.27 oz.) packet dry fajita seasoning
3 tbsp chopped fresh cilantro
16 oz. tortilla chips
8 oz. shredded Monterey Jack cheese

Directions

1. In a large pan, melt the margarine on medium heat and sauté the garlic and onion for about 5 minutes.
2. Stir in the flour and cook for about 1 minute, stirring continuously.
3. Stir in the broth and half-and-half and bring to a boil.
4. Reduce the heat to low and stir in the soup, salsa, corn, chicken, cumin, fajita seasoning and 2 tbsp of the cilantro.
5. Simmer for about 15 minutes.
6. In each serving bowl, place some crumbled tortilla chips and 1/2 oz. of the shredded cheese and top with the hot soup.
7. Serve with a topping of the more crumbled chips, remaining cheese and remaining cilantro

CHICKEN SOUP
Festival

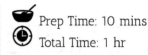 Prep Time: 10 mins
Total Time: 1 hr

Servings per Recipe: 8
Calories	290 kcal
Fat	16.3 g
Carbohydrates	13.8g
Protein	22 g
Cholesterol	74 mg
Sodium	512 mg

Ingredients

1 lb. skinless, boneless chicken breast halves
1 tbsp vegetable oil
1/2 C. diced onion
1 clove garlic, minced
1 quart chicken broth
1 C. masa harina
3 C. water, divided
1 C. enchilada sauce

2 C. shredded Cheddar cheese
1 tsp salt
1 tsp chili powder
1/2 tsp ground cumin

Directions

1. In a large pan, heat the oil on medium heat and cook the chicken breasts till well browned from all sides.
2. Transfer the chicken breasts into a bowl and keep aside.
3. After cooling, shred the chicken breasts.
4. In the same pan, add the onion and garlic and sauté till translucent.
5. Stir in the chicken broth.
6. In a bowl, add the masa harina and 2 C. of the water and beat till well combined.
7. In the pan of simmering broth, add the masa harina mixture, remaining 1 C. of the water, enchilada sauce, Cheddar, salt, chili powder and cumin and bring to a boil.
8. Add the shredded chicken and stir to combine.
9. Reduce the heat and simmer for about 30-40 minutes.
10. Serve hot.

Buffalo
Chicken Soup

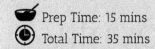 Prep Time: 15 mins
Total Time: 35 mins

Servings per Recipe: 8
Calories	259 kcal
Fat	18.3 g
Carbohydrates	6.9g
Protein	16.5 g
Cholesterol	72 mg
Sodium	570 mg

Ingredients

1/4 C. butter
3 stalks celery, diced
1 small onion, diced
1/4 C. all-purpose flour
3/4 C. half-and-half cream
3 C. water
1 cube chicken bouillon

2 C. cubed cooked chicken
1/4 C. buffalo wing sauce
1 1/2 C. shredded Cheddar cheese
Salt and pepper to taste

Directions

1. In a large pan, melt the butter on medium-high heat and sauté the celery and onion for about 5 minutes.
2. Stir in the flour and cook for about 2 minutes, stirring continuously.
3. Slowly, add the half-and-half and water and stir to combine.
4. Add the bouillon and stir to dissolve completely.
5. Stir in the chicken, buffalo wing sauce, Cheddar cheese, salt and pepper.
6. Reduce the heat to medium-low and simmer for about 10 minutes, stirring occasionally.

CHICKEN SOUP
Country

🍲 Prep Time: 20 mins
🕐 Total Time: 2 hrs 20 mins

Servings per Recipe: 8
Calories   562 kcal
Fat   25.2 g
Carbohydrates   45.3g
Protein   36.3 g
Cholesterol   223 mg
Sodium   648 mg

Ingredients

1 (2 to 3 lb.) whole chicken
2 (14.5 oz.) cans chicken broth
2 medium yellow onions, quartered
1 bunch of celery with leaves, cut into pieces
1 (16 oz.) package baby carrots
Salt and ground black pepper to taste

1/2 tsp garlic salt
5 eggs
1/2 C. water
1 tsp salt
3 C. all-purpose flour
1/2 tsp parsley flakes

Directions

1. In a large pan, add the chicken and enough water to cover.
2. Add the chicken broth, celery, onions, salt, pepper and garlic salt and bring to a boil.
3. Cook for about 1 hour.
4. Transfer the chicken onto a cutting board to cool.
5. Remove the meat from bones and chop the meat into pieces.
6. Discard the skin and bones.
7. Strain the broth and discard the celery and onions.
8. Return the broth to the pan and bring to a boil.
9. Stir in the carrots.
10. In a medium bowl, add the eggs, water and salt and beat till well combined.
11. Slowly, add the flour and mix till a ball like dough is formed.
12. Place the dough onto a flat plate and pat to smooth.
13. With a butter knife, cut the dough into 2-3-inch long slices.
14. Carefully, add the dough slices in the boiling broth and cook till the carrots become tender.
15. Serve with a sprinkling of the parsley flakes.

Central African Style Chicken Soup

Prep Time: 20 mins
Total Time: 40 mins

Servings per Recipe: 8
Calories	412 kcal
Fat	23 g
Carbohydrates	42.6g
Protein	11.5 g
Cholesterol	18 mg
Sodium	433 mg

Ingredients

1 tbsp vegetable oil
1 tsp chopped fresh ginger root
1 clove garlic, minced
2 tsp minced fresh Serrano or other small hot green chili, including seeds
2 chicken breasts cut into chunks
2 tsp red curry paste
1 tbsp curry powder
1 tbsp vinegar

1 tbsp fish sauce
2 tsp white sugar
2 C. chicken broth
2 (13.5 oz.) cans coconut milk
1 (20 oz.) can pineapple tidbits, drained
4 C. cooked rice

Directions

1. In a large pan, heat the oil on medium-high heat and cook the chicken, ginger, garlic and Serrano pepper for about 5 minutes.
2. Stir in the curry paste, curry powder, vinegar, fish sauce, sugar, chicken broth, coconut milk, pineapple and rice and simmer for about 15 minutes.

CHICKEN SOUP
with Rustic Root Vegetables

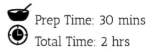

Prep Time: 30 mins
Total Time: 2 hrs

Servings per Recipe: 12	
Calories	209 kcal
Fat	8.5 g
Carbohydrates	15.5g
Protein	18.6 g
Cholesterol	50 mg
Sodium	376 mg

Ingredients

1 whole chicken, quartered
Water, to cover
1/2 large onion, chopped
1 stalk of celery with leaves, cut into chunks
3 cubes chicken bouillon
1/4 C. chopped fresh basil
1/4 C. chopped fresh parsley
1 tbsp chopped garlic
1 pinch salt and ground black pepper to taste
2 Yukon Gold potatoes, diced
2 kohlrabi bulbs, peeled and diced
2 carrots, sliced
1 large turnip, diced
1/2 medium head cabbage, chopped
2 ears sweet corn, cut from cob
4 oz. fresh green beans, trimmed
1 tomato, chopped

Directions

1. In a large pan, add the chicken pieces and enough water to cover completely on medium-high heat.
2. Add the onion, celery, bouillon cubes, basil, parsley, garlic, salt and pepper and bring to a boil.
3. Reduce the heat and simmer for about 1 hour.
4. Discard the celery chunks.
5. Transfer the chicken onto a cutting board to cool.
6. Remove the meat from bones and chop the meat roughly.
7. Discard the skin and bones.
8. In the pan, add the chopped chicken, potatoes, kohlrabi, carrots and turnip and cook for about 20 minutes.
9. Stir in the cabbage, corn, green beans and tomato and cook for about 7-10 minutes.

Brown Rice
Chicken Soup

🥣 Prep Time: 15 mins
🕐 Total Time: 1 hr 55 mins

Servings per Recipe: 10
Calories	101 kcal
Fat	1.2 g
Carbohydrates	15.4g
Protein	6.8 g
Cholesterol	14 mg
Sodium	759 mg

Ingredients

5 C. chicken broth
2 skinless, boneless chicken breast halves
1 C. diced celery
1 C. diced onion
1/4 C. diced carrots
1/4 C. corn
1/4 C. drained and rinsed black beans
1 tsp dried sage

1 tsp ground black pepper
1 tsp salt
1 bay leaf
3/4 C. brown rice

Directions

1. In a large pan, add the chicken broth and bring to a boil.
2. Add the chicken breasts and cook for about 20 minutes.
3. Transfer the chicken breast into a bowl and keep aside to cool.
4. Remove the meat from bones and with 2 forks, shred the meat.
5. Discard the skin and bones.
6. In the simmering broth, add the shredded chicken, celery, onion, carrots, corn, black beans, sage, pepper, salt and bay leaves and cook for about 20 minutes.
7. Stir in the brown rice and simmer for about 1 hour.

WESTERN EUROPEAN
Style Chicken Soup

🥣 Prep Time: 35 mins
🕐 Total Time: 1 hr 10 mins

Servings per Recipe: 4
Calories	159 kcal
Fat	7.1 g
Carbohydrates	6.8g
Protein	16.8 g
Cholesterol	49 mg
Sodium	63 mg

Ingredients

1 whole bone-in chicken breast, with skin
1 onion, cut into thin wedges
4 sprigs fresh parsley
1/2 tsp lemon zest
1 sprig fresh mint
6 C. chicken stock

1/3 C. thin egg noodles
2 tbsp chopped fresh mint leaves
Salt to taste
1/4 tsp freshly ground white pepper

Directions

1. In a large pan, add the chicken breast, stock, onion, parsley, lemon zest and mint sprig and simmer for about 35 minutes.
2. Transfer the chicken breast into a bowl and keep aside to cool.
3. Remove the meat from bones and cut into bite-size pieces.
4. Discard the skin and bones.
5. Strain the broth and return to the pan and bring to a boil.
6. Stir in the pasta, chopped mint, salt and white pepper and cook till the pasta is cooked to desired doneness.
7. Remove from the heat and immediately, stir in the lemon juice and chopped chicken.
8. Serve hot with a topping of the lemon slice and mint leaf.

Nutty Potato
Chicken Soup

🥣 Prep Time: 35 mins

🕐 Total Time: 1 hr 10 mins

Servings per Recipe: 12

Calories	275 kcal
Fat	12 g
Carbohydrates	27.1g
Protein	16 g
Cholesterol	31 mg
Sodium	62 mg

Ingredients

1 C. slivered almonds

2 tbsp olive oil

1 medium onion, chopped

1 C. chopped celery

4 C. sliced fresh mushrooms

4 cloves garlic, minced

1 C. chopped carrots

5 C. diced red potatoes

3 C. chopped cooked chicken

2 1/2 quarts chicken broth

1 C. quick-cooking barley

2 tbsp butter

1/2 C. chopped fresh parsley

Salt and black pepper to taste

Directions

1. Set your oven to 400 degrees F before doing anything else.
2. Place the slivered almonds onto a baking sheet evenly.
3. Cook in the oven till golden brown and fragrant.
4. In a large pan, heat the oil on medium heat and cook the onions, celery, mushrooms and garlic till tender.
5. Stir in the carrots, potatoes, chicken and broth and bring to a boil.
6. Add the barley and stir to combine.
7. Reduce the heat and simmer, covered for about 20 minutes.
8. Remove from the heat and stir in the butter, parsley, toasted almonds, salt and pepper and remove from the heat.
9. Serve hot.

JAPANESE INSPIRED
Bamboo and Mushroom Chicken Soup

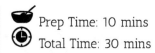

Prep Time: 10 mins
Total Time: 30 mins

Servings per Recipe: 4
Calories	203 kcal
Fat	7.3 g
Carbohydrates	8.4g
Protein	25.9 g
Cholesterol	105 mg
Sodium	222 mg

Ingredients

3 C. chicken broth
1/2 C. water
2 C. sliced fresh mushrooms
1/2 C. sliced bamboo shoots, drained
3 slices fresh ginger root
2 cloves garlic, crushed
2 tsp soy sauce
1/4 tsp red pepper flakes
1 lb. skinless, boneless chicken breast halves - cut into thin strips

1 tbsp sesame oil
2 green onions, chopped
1/4 C. chopped fresh cilantro
3 tbsp red wine vinegar
2 tbsp cornstarch
1 egg, beaten

Directions

1. In a pan, add the chicken broth, water, mushrooms, bamboo shoots, ginger, garlic, soy sauce and hot pepper flakes and bring to a boil.
2. Reduce the heat to low and simmer, covered till the preparation of remaining
3. Ingredients
4. In a bowl, add the chicken slices and sesame oil and toss to coat.
5. In another bowl, dissolve the cornstarch in vinegar.
6. Increase the heat under the broth to medium-high and bring to a rolling boil.
7. Add the chicken slices and again, bring to a boil.
8. Drizzle the egg, stirring slowly.
9. Stir in the cornstarch and reduce the heat to medium.
10. Simmer for about 3 minutes, stirring occasionally.
11. Serve hot with a garnishing of the green onions and cilantro.

Arizona
Inspired Chicken Soup

Prep Time: 15 mins
Total Time: 1 hr 40 mins

Servings per Recipe: 9
Calories	304 kcal
Fat	11.3 g
Carbohydrates	24.6g
Protein	24.9 g
Cholesterol	67 mg
Sodium	371 mg

Ingredients

1 (3 lb.) whole chicken, cut into pieces
4 quarts water
3 stalks celery, chopped
2 cloves garlic
1 onion, finely diced
2 (14 oz.) cans peeled and diced tomatoes with juice
2 cubes chicken bouillon
1 red bell pepper, chopped
1/2 tsp ground cumin

1/4 tsp ground cayenne pepper
1/4 tsp ground white pepper
1 (10 oz.) package frozen corn kernels
1 bunch green onions, thinly sliced
2 bunches chopped fresh cilantro
2 C. cooked white rice
Salt to taste

Directions

1. In a large pan, add the chicken, water, onion, celery and garlic and bring to a boil.
2. Reduce the heat and simmer, covered for about 45 minutes.
3. Transfer the chicken into a bowl and keep aside to cool.
4. Remove the meat from bones and cut into bite-size pieces.
5. Discard the skin and bones.
6. Skim off the fat from the broth.
7. With the back of a spoon, smash the cooked garlic cloves against the side of the pan.
8. Add the tomatoes with juice, cumin, cayenne pepper, white pepper and bouillon cube and simmer, covered for about 30 minutes.
9. Stir in the corn, green onion and cilantro and simmer for about 10 minutes.
10. Add the chicken and cooked rice and cook till heated completely.
11. Stir in the salt and remove from the heat.
12. Serve hot with a garnishing of the cheese and tortilla chips.

PENNSYLVANIAN
Dutch Style Chicken Soup with Rivels

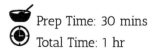 Prep Time: 30 mins
Total Time: 1 hr

Servings per Recipe: 12
Calories   271 kcal
Fat   12.4 g
Carbohydrates   14.2g
Protein   24.7 g
Cholesterol   118 mg
Sodium   90 mg

Ingredients

1 (4 lb.) chicken
1 onion, chopped
4 quarts water
1 (10 oz.) package frozen whole kernel corn
1/2 C. chopped celery
Salt and pepper to taste

1 C. all-purpose flour
1 pinch salt
1 egg
1/4 C. milk
2 hard-cooked eggs, chopped

Directions

1. In a large pan, add chicken, onion and water and cook slowly for about 1 hour.
2. Transfer the chicken into a bowl and keep aside to cool.
3. Remove the meat from bones and cut into 1-inch pieces.
4. Discard the skin and bones.
5. Add corn, chopped chicken, celery, salt and pepper and simmer for about 10 minutes.
6. For the rivels in a bowl, add flour, salt, egg and enough milk and mix till small crumbs form.
7. Carefully, place the rivels and hard boiled eggs and simmer for about 15 minutes.
8. Serve hot.
9. NOTE: Rivels are type of dumpling alternative used to enhance liquids.

Ramen Noodle
Chicken Soup

🥣 Prep Time: 5 mins
🕐 Total Time: 25 mins

Servings per Recipe: 4

Calories	111 kcal
Fat	4 g
Carbohydrates	7.4g
Protein	11.6 g
Cholesterol	31 mg
Sodium	1057 mg

Ingredients

3 1/2 C. Swanson(R) Chicken Broth
1 tsp soy sauce
1 tsp ground ginger
1 dash black pepper
1 medium carrot, sliced diagonally
1 stalk celery, sliced diagonally
1/2 red bell pepper, cut into 2-inch-long strips
2 green onions, sliced diagonally
1 clove garlic, minced
4 oz. broken-up uncooked ramen noodles
1 C. cooked, shredded boneless, skinless chicken breast meat

Directions

1. In a large pan, add the broth, soy sauce, ginger, black pepper, carrot, celery, red pepper, green onions and garlic on medium-high heat and bring to a boil.
2. Add the noodles and chicken and stir to combine.
3. Reduce the heat to medium and cook for about 10 minutes.

LATE SEPTEMBER'S
Best Chicken Soup

Prep Time: 20 mins
Total Time: 20 mins

Servings per Recipe: 4
Calories	470 kcal
Fat	25.5 g
Carbohydrates	23.2g
Protein	36.9 g
Cholesterol	139 mg
Sodium	427 mg

Ingredients

1 1/2 C. small broccoli florets
1 C. sliced fresh mushrooms
1/2 C. shredded carrot
1/4 C. chopped onion
1/4 C. butter
1/4 C. all-purpose flour
1/2 tsp dried basil, crushed
1/4 tsp black pepper
3 C. milk

1 C. half-and-half or light cream
1 1/2 tsp Worcestershire sauce
1 1/2 tsp instant chicken bouillon granules
2 (6 oz.) packages Tyson(R) Grilled & Ready(R) Refrigerated Diced Chicken Breast

Directions

1. In a large pan, melt the butter and cook the broccoli, mushrooms, carrot and onion for about 6-8 minutes.

2. Stir in the flour, basil, pepper, milk, half-and-half, Worcestershire sauce and bouillon granules and cook till the mixture becomes thick.

3. Stir in the chicken and cook till heated completely.

Full-Ingredient
Chicken Soup

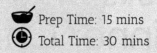
Prep Time: 15 mins
Total Time: 30 mins

Servings per Recipe: 6
Calories	508 kcal
Fat	45 g
Carbohydrates	14.5g
Protein	13.3 g
Cholesterol	141 mg
Sodium	1590 mg

Ingredients

3 tbsp olive oil
1 small onion, diced
1 (4 oz.) can diced green chilis
1 (14.5 oz.) can fire-roasted diced tomatoes, undrained
8 oz. cream cheese
1 1/2 C. Swanson(R) Unsalted Chicken Broth
1 1/2 C. heavy cream
2 tsp lemon juice
3 tsp garlic powder

2 tsp salt
2 tsp cumin
1 tsp onion salt
2 pinches cayenne pepper
1 C. shredded cooked chicken
1 bunch green onions, white part only, chopped
4 tbsp chopped fresh cilantro
1 C. crushed tortilla chips, for garnish

Directions

1. In a large pan, heat the oil on medium heat and sauté the onion till translucent.
2. Add the green chilies and diced tomatoes and cook till half of the liquid absorbs, stirring continuously.
3. Add the cream cheese and cook for about 3-5 minutes, stirring continuously.
4. Stir in the broth, cream, lemon juice, garlic powder, salt, cumin, onion salt, cayenne, shredded chicken and cook till heated completely.
5. Serve with a garnishing of the chopped green onions, chopped cilantro and crushed tortilla chips.

THURSDAY NIGHT
er Chicken
Soup

Prep Time: 25 mins
Total Time: 1 hr 10 mins

Servings per Recipe: 7
Calories	572 kcal
Fat	30.1 g
Carbohydrates	41.4g
Protein	35.9 g
Cholesterol	119 mg
Sodium	1186 mg

Ingredients

10 slices turkey bacon, cut into 1-inch pieces
2 tbsp butter
1 C. diced yellow onion
1 C. diced red bell pepper
1 large jalapeño chili pepper, diced
1 large clove garlic, minced
1/4 C. all-purpose flour
1 1/2 tsp kosher salt
1/2 tsp ground black pepper
1/2 tsp ground cumin
1/2 tsp chili powder
1 pinch cayenne pepper
5 C. Swanson(R) Unsalted Chicken Broth

3 1/2 C. Yukon gold potatoes, 3/4-inch dice
1 (4 oz.) can chopped green chilis, drained
3 C. frozen corn
3 C. chopped rotisserie chicken
2 C. half-and-half
1 C. grated sharp Cheddar cheese
Garnishes:
1/2 C. grated sharp Cheddar cheese
1/4 C. chopped fresh cilantro leaves
1/4 C. chopped green onion

Directions

1. Heat a Dutch oven on medium-high heat and cook the bacon for about 10 minutes, turning occasionally.
2. Transfer the bacon onto a paper towel lined plate to drain.
3. Drain off the bacon grease, leaving only 2 tbsp in the pan.
4. In the same, pan; melt the butter with the bacon grease on medium heat and sauté the onion, red bell pepper and jalapeño pepper for about 5-6 minutes.
5. Add the minced garlic and sauté for about 1 minute.
6. Add the flour and cook for about 2 minutes, beating continuously.
7. Stir in the salt, pepper, cumin, chili powder and cayenne pepper.
8. Slowly, add the broth, stirring continuously.

9. Bring to a boil on medium-high heat and stir in the potatoes and green chilies.

10. Reduce the heat to medium-low and simmer for about 12 minutes.

11. Stir in the frozen corn, chopped chicken, 1/2 C. of the cooked bacon pieces and half-and-half.

12. Reduce the heat to low and simmer very slowly for about 8-10 minutes.

13. Remove from the heat and stir in 1 C. of the grated Cheddar cheese till melted completely.

14. Serve hot with a garnishing of the reserved bacon, grated Cheddar cheese, cilantro, and green onions

ALTERNATIVE
Asian Chicken Soup

Prep Time: 20 mins
Total Time: 1 hr 30 mins

Servings per Recipe: 8
Calories	396 kcal
Fat	15.4 g
Carbohydrates	29.1g
Protein	33 g
Cholesterol	101 mg
Sodium	1118 mg

Ingredients

3 lb. chicken leg quarters
3 (32 oz.) cartons low-sodium chicken broth
1 tbsp Hawaiian sea salt
1 (1/2 inch) piece fresh ginger root, sliced
1 large Maui sweet onion, cubed

1 (8 oz.) package uncooked bean threads (cellophane noodles)
1 bunch green onions, thinly sliced
1 small head bok Choy, chopped

Directions

1. In a large pan, add the chicken, chicken broth, salt and ginger on high heat and bring to a boil.
2. Reduce the heat to medium-low and simmer for about 35 minutes.
3. Transfer the chicken into a bowl.
4. Remove the skin and bones from the chicken and chop the meat roughly.
5. Discard the skin and bones.
6. Strain the broth into another and discard the solids.
7. In a large bowl of the hot water, soak the long rice noodles for about 30 minutes.
8. Add the onion in the broth and bring to a boil.
9. Reduce the heat to medium-low and stir in the noodles, chicken meat, green onion and bok Choy.
10. Simmer till the noodles become tender.
11. Serve hot.

Manhattan Island
Chicken Soup

🥣 Prep Time: 15 mins
🕐 Total Time: 4 hrs 15 mins

Servings per Recipe: 8

Calories	525 kcal
Fat	27.2 g
Carbohydrates	39.5g
Protein	32.1 g
Cholesterol	212 mg
Sodium	721 mg

Ingredients

1 whole chicken
1 medium yellow onion, chopped
8 carrots, peeled and sliced
1 parsnip, chopped
3 cloves garlic, crushed
2 stalks celery, chopped
1 bunch fresh dill weed, chopped

Salt and pepper to taste
2 1/2 C. matzo meal
6 eggs
6 tbsp vegetable oil
2 tsp salt

Directions

1. In a large pan, place the chicken, breast side down on medium heat.
2. Add enough cold water to reach about 3-inch from the top of the pan.
3. Add the onion, carrot, parsnip, celery and dill and bring to a gentle boil.
4. Simmer, covered partially for about 2 hours, skimming any fat from the top of the soup occasionally
5. Add the garlic cloves and simmer, covered partially for about 2 hours.
6. With a slotted spoon, transfer about 1/4 C. of the broth from the soup into a bowl.
7. In the bowl, add the matzo meal, eggs, oil and salt and mix till well combined.
8. Refrigerate for about 20 minutes.
9. Remove from the refrigerator and with wet hands, make 16 equal sized balls from the matzo dough.
10. In another pan of the boiling, add the matzo balls and cook, covered for about 35 minutes.
11. Through a strainer, strain the broth from the chicken soup.
12. Return the broth to the pan. Remove the bones and skin from the chicken and cut into pieces. Remove the matzo balls from the water.
13. Add the shredded chicken and matzo balls in the simmering broth and serve hot.

CHICKEN SOUP
Sampler

Prep Time: 30 mins
Total Time: 1 hr 30 mins

Servings per Recipe: 6

Calories	101 kcal
Fat	5.6 g
Carbohydrates	10.2g
Protein	3.3 g
Cholesterol	72 mg
Sodium	252 mg

Ingredients

2 eggs, lightly beaten
2 tbsp melted butter
1/2 C. matzo meal
1 tsp chopped fresh flat-leaf parsley
1/2 tsp salt
1 dash white pepper
1 tbsp water

6 C. chicken broth
1 medium carrot, cut into 2 inch julienne strips

Directions

1. In a small bowl, add the eggs, melted butter and beat till well combined.
2. Add the matzo meal, parsley, salt, pepper and water and mix till soft dough is formed.
3. Refrigerate, covered for at least 30 minutes.
4. In a large pan, add the chicken broth and carrots and bring to a boil.
5. Reduce the heat to a simmer.
6. With wet hands, make 12 equal sized balls from the matzo dough.
7. Carefully, place the matzo balls in the simmering broth and simmer, covered for about 30-40 minutes.

Chicken Soup
with Garden Salsa

🥣 Prep Time: 10 mins

🕐 Total Time: 5 hrs 10 mins

Servings per Recipe: 8

Calories	179 kcal
Fat	3.4 g
Carbohydrates	12.4g
Protein	23.9 g
Cholesterol	59 mg
Sodium	1230 mg

Ingredients

Chicken:

4 large skinless, boneless chicken breasts

1 tbsp cumin

1 tsp ground black pepper

1 tsp adobo seasoning

1/2 lime, juiced

Salsa:

6 tomatillos, husked and chopped

3 Serrano chilis, stemmed

1 onion, chopped

3 garlic cloves, peeled

1 bunch cilantro

1 tbsp kosher salt

Soup:

1 (32 fluid oz.) container chicken stock

1 (15.5 oz.) can white hominy, drained

Directions

1. In a slow cooker, place the chicken breasts.
2. Set the slow cooker on Low and cook, covered for about 4 1/2 hours.
3. Remove the chicken breasts from the slow cooker.
4. Shred the chicken and transfer into a large pan.
5. Add the cumin, black pepper, adobo seasoning and lime juice and mix till well combined.
6. In a clear microwave-safe bag, place the tomatillos and Serrano peppers.
7. Seal the bag and with a knife, pierce a few times to vent.
8. Microwave for about 4-5 minutes
9. In a blender, add the softened tomatillos, Serrano peppers, onion, garlic, cilantro and salt and pulse till the salsa Verde becomes smooth.
10. In the pan of the chicken, add the chicken stock, hominy and half of the salsa Verde on medium heat and simmer for about 30 minutes.

6-INGREDIENT
Creamy Chicken Soup

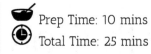 Prep Time: 10 mins
Total Time: 25 mins

Servings per Recipe: 4
Calories   327 kcal
Fat   25.8 g
Carbohydrates   10.6g
Protein   12.9 g
Cholesterol   96 mg
Sodium   882 mg

Ingredients

6 tbsp butter
1/3 C. all-purpose flour
3 C. chicken broth
1/2 C. milk

1/2 C. light cream
1 C. finely chopped cooked chicken

Directions

1. In a large pan, melt the butter on medium-high heat.
2. Add the flour and beat till a smooth paste is formed.
3. Add the chicken broth, milk and light cream and beat till well combined.
4. Bring to a boil and cook for about 5-10 minutes.
5. Reduce the heat to medium and stir in the cooked chicken.
6. Again, bring to a boil and cook for about 5-10 minutes.

Chicken Soup
Dublin Inspired

Prep Time: 20 mins
Total Time: 1 hr 10 mins

Servings per Recipe: 12
Calories	201 kcal
Fat	6.7 g
Carbohydrates	25.5g
Protein	9.5 g
Cholesterol	11 mg
Sodium	1055 mg

Ingredients

5 medium red potatoes, cubed
1/4 C. olive oil
3 stalks celery, diced
3 carrots, peeled and diced
1 onion, diced
2 garlic cloves, minced
2 tsp salt
2 tsp ground black pepper

6 C. chicken broth
2 C. skim milk
1 head cauliflower, cut into small florets
2 cooked chicken breasts, shredded
1 C. grated, reduced fat Parmesan cheese

Directions

1. Set your oven to 425 degrees F before doing anything else and lightly, grease a baking sheet.
2. Arrange the potatoes onto the prepared baking sheet.
3. Cook in the oven for about 30 minutes.
4. In a large pan, heat the olive oil on medium heat and cook the celery, carrots, onion, garlic, salt and pepper for about 10 minutes.
5. Stir in the chicken broth and milk and bring to a boil.
6. Add the cauliflower and stir to combine.
7. Reduce the heat to medium and cook for about 10 minutes.
8. Stir in the potatoes, chicken and Parmesan cheese and simmer for about 20 minutes.

60-MINUTE
Chicken Soup

Prep Time: 15 mins
Total Time: 1 hr

Servings per Recipe: 6

Calories	489 kcal
Fat	29.5 g
Carbohydrates	38.9g
Protein	20.2 g
Cholesterol	48 mg
Sodium	1394 mg

Ingredients

1 quart oil for frying
3 lb. chicken drumettes
2 (26 oz.) cans condensed tomato soup
6 C. water

2 green bell peppers, diced
1 large Vidalia onion, diced

Directions

1. In a large, heavy skillet, heat the oil to 375 degrees and fry the drumettes till golden brown from all sides.
2. Transfer the drumettes into a bowl and drain the excess oil.
3. In a large pan, add the tomato soup and water and bring to a boil.
4. Stir in the drumettes, green bell peppers and Vidalia onion
5. Reduce the heat and stir in the drumettes, green bell peppers and Vidalia onion.
6. Simmer for about 15 minutes.
7. Serve hot.

Grocery Rotisserie
Orzo Chicken Soup

🥣 Prep Time: 15 mins

🕐 Total Time: 55 mins

Servings per Recipe: 5

Calories	514 kcal
Fat	11.4 g
Carbohydrates	70.4g
Protein	31.2 g
Cholesterol	65 mg
Sodium	1859 mg

Ingredients

2 (32 oz.) cartons chicken broth
1/2 cooked rotisserie chicken, meat removed from bones and chopped
1 C. sliced carrots
1 Macintosh apple, cored and diced
1/2 onion, diced

1/2 C. sliced celery
1/4 C. grated Parmesan cheese
1 bay leaf
2 C. orzo pasta

Directions

1. In a large pan, add the chicken broth, chicken, carrots, apple, onion, celery, Parmesan cheese and bay leaf and bring to a boil.
2. Reduce the heat to medium-low and simmer for about 30 minutes.
3. Stir in the orzo and cook for about 11 minutes, stirring occasionally.

30-MINUTE
Mediterranean Chicken Soup

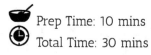 Prep Time: 10 mins
Total Time: 30 mins

Servings per Recipe: 15
Calories	323 kcal
Fat	13.5 g
Carbohydrates	23.8g
Protein	24.4 g
Cholesterol	69 mg
Sodium	2011 mg

Ingredients

2 (48 oz.) containers chicken broth
4 (12 oz.) cans chicken chunks, drained
1 1/2 C. white rice
2 (26 oz.) cans cream of chicken soup

3/4 C. lemon juice

Directions

1. In a pan, add the chicken broth and canned chicken and bring to a boil.
2. Stir in the rice and simmer for about 15-20 minutes.
3. Stir in the cream of chicken soup and lemon juice and simmer for about 5-10 minutes, stirring occasionally.

Upstate NY Inspired Chicken Soup

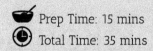 Prep Time: 15 mins

Total Time: 35 mins

Servings per Recipe: 8

Calories	294 kcal
Fat	21.5 g
Carbohydrates	8.1g
Protein	16.8 g
Cholesterol	78 mg
Sodium	863 mg

Ingredients

1/4 C. butter
3 stalks celery, diced
1 small onion, diced
1/4 C. all-purpose flour
2 C. chicken broth
1 C. water
3/4 C. half-and-half
2 C. cubed, cooked chicken

1 1/2 C. shredded Cheddar cheese
1/3 C. buffalo wing sauce
1/4 C. creamy tomato soup
Salt and ground black pepper to taste
1/4 C. crumbled blue cheese

Directions

1. In a large pan, melt the butter on medium-high heat and sauté the celery and onion for about 5 minutes.
2. Sprinkle flour over the soup and cook for about 2 minutes, stirring continuously.
3. Slowly, add the chicken broth, water and half-and-half, stirring continuously.
4. Stir in the Cheddar cheese, buffalo wing sauce and tomato soup and bring to a gentle boil, stirring occasionally.
5. Cook for about 10 minutes.
6. Serve hot with a topping of the blue cheese crumbles.

I ♥ Chicken Soup

🍲 Prep Time: 25 mins
🕐 Total Time: 35 mins

Servings per Recipe: 4
Calories	288 kcal
Fat	13.9 g
Carbohydrates	22.9 g
Protein	18.4 g
Cholesterol	59 mg
Sodium	1033 mg

Ingredients

3 C. chicken broth
2 cloves garlic, minced
1 1/2 tbsp unsalted butter
3/4 tsp white sugar
1 carrot, thinly sliced
1 stalk celery, thinly sliced
1 C. potato gnocchi
4 oz. frozen peas
4 oz. frozen corn

1 C. shredded cooked chicken
2 oz. baby spinach
Salt and freshly ground black pepper to taste
1/2 C. grated Parmesan cheese

Directions

1. In a large pan, add the broth, garlic, butter and sugar and bring to a gentle boil.
2. Cook for about 2 minutes.
3. Stir in the carrot and celery and bring to a boil.
4. Stir in the gnocchi and cook for about 2-3 minutes.
5. Add the peas and corn and cook for about 30 seconds.
6. Stir in the chicken, spinach, salt and black pepper and remove from the heat.
7. Serve hot with a topping of the Parmesan cheese.

Tuesday's
Spicy Chicken Ramen Noodle Soup

🍲 Prep Time: 10 mins
🕐 Total Time: 35 mins

Servings per Recipe: 8

Calories	165 kcal
Fat	8.5 g
Carbohydrates	6g
Protein	16.5 g
Cholesterol	43 mg
Sodium	568 mg

Ingredients

2 tbsp sesame oil
1/2 tsp ground turmeric
2 tsp chopped fresh ginger root
2 tbsp chili paste
1 lb. chopped cooked chicken breast
1 quart chicken broth
2 tsp sugar
1/4 C. soy sauce

1 C. chopped celery
1 (3 oz.) package ramen noodles
1 C. shredded lettuce
1/2 C. chopped green onion

Directions

1. In a large pan, heat the oil on medium heat and sauté the turmeric, ginger and chili paste for about 1-2 minutes.
2. Stir in the chicken, broth, sugar, soy sauce and celery and bring to a boil.
3. Stir in the noodles and cook for about 3 minutes.
4. Stir in the lettuce and remove from the heat.
5. Serve with a garnishing of the green onions.

CHICKEN
and Rice Soup

Prep Time: 10 mins
Total Time: 40 mins

Servings per Recipe: 5

Calories	121 kcal
Fat	0.6 g
Carbohydrates	< 26.4g
Protein	3 g
Cholesterol	< 1 mg
Sodium	< 536 mg

Ingredients

6 C. water
1 C. uncooked white rice
1 small onion, chopped
2 tbsp chicken bouillon granules
1 tbsp dried parsley
1 pinch garlic powder

2 (14.5 oz.) cans stewed tomatoes
1 (10.5 oz.) can condensed chicken rice soup

Directions

1. In a large pan, add the water, rice, onion, bouillon granules, and parsley and garlic powder and bring to a boil.
2. Reduce the heat and simmer for about 20 minutes.
3. Stir in the tomatoes and chicken and bring to a boil.

30-Minute 5-Ingredient Store Bought Chicken Soup

Prep Time: 5 mins
Total Time: 30 mins

Servings per Recipe: 4
Calories	281 kcal
Fat	4.1 g
Carbohydrates	43.2g
Protein	16.5 g
Cholesterol	31 mg
Sodium	1477 mg

Ingredients

3 1/2 C. Swanson(R) Chicken Broth
1/2 C. uncooked long grain white rice
1 (16 oz.) can Beans

1/2 C. Pace(R) Chunky Salsa
1 C. cubed cooked chicken

Directions

1. In a large pan, add the broth on medium-high heat and bring to a boil.
2. Add the rice and stir to combine.
3. Reduce the heat to low and simmer, covered for about 20 minutes.
4. Stir the beans, salsa and chicken and cook till heated completely.

CREAMY
Chicken Soup

Prep Time: 5 mins
Total Time: 30 mins

Servings per Recipe: 8
Calories	361 kcal
Fat	12.3 g
Carbohydrates	42.5g
Protein	21.4 g
Cholesterol	64 mg
Sodium	584 mg

Ingredients

1 (4.5 oz.) package quick cooking wild
rice and chicken flavor mix
2 boneless chicken breast halves,
cooked and cubed
3 C. chicken broth
1 (16 oz.) package frozen pearl onions

1 C. sliced mushrooms
1 stalk celery, diced
2 tbsp chopped fresh parsley
Salt and pepper to taste
1 C. half-and-half cream

Directions

1. Cook the rice mix according to packages
2. Directions
3. In a large pan, add 1 1/2 C. of the cooked rice mix, cooked chicken, broth, onions, mushrooms, celery, parsley, salt and pepper and bring to a boil.
4. Reduce the heat and simmer for about 20 minutes.
5. Stir in the half-and-half and cook for about 5 minutes, stirring occasionally.

Chicken Soup
Clásico

🥣 Prep Time: 30 mins
🕐 Total Time: 2 hrs 30 mins

Servings per Recipe: 6
Calories	1554 kcal
Fat	105 g
Carbohydrates	48.8g
Protein	96.5 g
Cholesterol	363 mg
Sodium	705 mg

Ingredients

3 (3 lb.) whole chicken
4 C. diced celery
2 C. chopped onion
1 tsp salt
3 C. all-purpose flour
3 C. frozen corn

Salt to taste
Ground white pepper
1 tbsp dried parsley

Directions

1. In a large pan, add the chicken, celery and enough water to cover and bring to a boil.
2. Simmer for about 2 hours.
3. Transfer the chicken into a bowl and keep aside to cool.
4. Reserve 2 C. of the chicken broth into a bowl and keep aside to cool.
5. After cooing, remove and discard the skin and bones.
6. Chop the chicken meat and return to the pan.
7. In a food processor, add the flour and 1 tsp of the salt.
8. While the motor is running slowly, add the reserved chicken broth through the opening in the lid and pulse till a ball like dough is formed.
9. Transfer the dough into a bowl and keep aside for about 20 minutes.
10. Place the dough onto a lightly floured surface and roll into 1/4-inch thickness.
11. Cut the dough into thin strips and then cut each strip into pieces to form short thin noodles.
12. Again bring the broth to a boil and stir in the noodles and corn.
13. Cook for about 10 minutes.
14. Stir in the salt and pepper and remove from the heat.
15. Serve hot with a garnishing of the parsley flakes.

SPICIER
Chicken Soup

Prep Time: 20 mins
Total Time: 48 mins

Servings per Recipe: 6
Calories	153 kcal
Fat	3.1 g
Carbohydrates	5.4g
Protein	25 g
Cholesterol	64 mg
Sodium	1125 mg

Ingredients

4 C. chicken broth
2 C. water
1/4 C. finely chopped onion
1 small jalapeno pepper, seeded and minced
1 (1 inch) piece fresh ginger root, finely chopped
2 cloves garlic
1 lb. boneless, skinless chicken breasts
1 head bok Choy, chopped
Salt to taste

Directions

1. In a large pan, add the chicken broth, water, onion, jalapeño, ginger and garlic and bring to a boil.
2. Add the chicken breasts and cook for about 15-20 minutes.
3. Transfer the chicken into a bowl and keep aside to cool for about 5 minutes.
4. With 2 forks, shred the chicken.
5. In the pan of soup, stir in the chicken, bok Choy and cook for about 3-5 minutes.
6. Stir in the salt and serve.

Saturday Night
Chicken Soup

Prep Time: 10 mins
Total Time: 35 mins

Servings per Recipe: 8

Calories	427 kcal
Fat	22.9 g
Carbohydrates	29.4g
Protein	25.2 g
Cholesterol	95 mg
Sodium	740 mg

Ingredients

1/4 C. onion, diced
1 tbsp bacon grease
3 C. 1-inch potato chunks
2 C. chicken broth
1 C. water
3 tbsp butter

3 tbsp flour
1 C. milk
3 oz. shredded Cheddar cheese
1 1/2 C. shredded cooked chicken

Directions

1. In a large pan, heat the bacon grease on medium-high heat and sauté the onion for about 4 minutes.
2. Stir in the potato chunks, chicken broth and water and bring to a boil.
3. Cook for about 15 minutes.
4. Meanwhile in a small pan, melt the butter on medium heat.
5. Stir in the flour and cook for about 1 minute, stirring continuously.
6. Add milk and cook for about 3 minutes, stirring continuously.
7. Stir in the cheese and cook for about 2-3 minutes, stirring continuously.
8. Add the cheese mixture and cooked chicken into the simmering soup and cook for about 4 minutes.

CHICKEN SOUP
Thai Style

Prep Time: 15 mins
Total Time: 30 mins

Servings per Recipe: 6

Calories	436 kcal
Fat	25.6 g
Carbohydrates	32g
Protein	26.7 g
Cholesterol	49 mg
Sodium	1477 mg

Ingredients

1 C. coconut milk
2 lemon grass, chopped
4 slices (1/2-inch) piece peeled fresh ginger
5 kaffir lime leaves, torn in half
3/4 lb. skinless, boneless chicken breasts cut into strips
5 tbsp fish sauce

2 tbsp white sugar
1 C. coconut milk
1/2 C. lime juice
1 tsp red curry paste
1/4 C. coarsely chopped cilantro
15 green chilis, crushed

Directions

1. In a large pan, add 1 C. of the coconut milk, lemon grass, ginger, and kaffir lime leaves on medium-high heat and bring to a boil.
2. Stir in the chicken, fish sauce and sugar.
3. Reduce heat to medium and cook for about 5 minutes.
4. Stir in the remaining 1 C. of the coconut milk and bring to a simmer.
5. In 4 serving bowls, divide the lime juice and curry paste and top with hot soup.
6. Serve with a garnishing of the cilantro and Thai chilis.

New Mexico
Chicken Soup

🍲 Prep Time: 15 mins

🕐 Total Time: 35 mins

Servings per Recipe: 12

Calories	123 kcal
Fat	2.4 g
Carbohydrates	14.9g
Protein	10.6 g
Cholesterol	17 mg
Sodium	956 mg

Ingredients

32 oz. chicken broth

2 (15 oz.) cans black beans, rinsed and drained

1 (14 oz.) can diced tomatoes with green chili peppers

1 (14 oz.) can petite diced tomatoes

2 (6 oz.) cans chunk white chicken, drained

1 tbsp minced garlic

1/2 tsp red pepper flakes

Salt and ground black pepper to taste

Directions

1. In a large pan, add all the

2. Ingredients and bring to a simmer.

3. Simmer for about 20 minutes.

4. Serve hot.

CREAM
of Chicken Soup

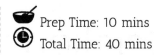
Prep Time: 10 mins
Total Time: 40 mins

Servings per Recipe: 4
Calories   529 kcal
Fat   29 g
Carbohydrates   39.9g
Protein   28.4 g
Cholesterol   113 mg
Sodium   1645 mg

Ingredients

1/2 lb. chicken breast, cut into bite-sized pieces
1 (14.5 oz.) can chicken broth
1 (9 oz.) package refrigerated cheese tortellini
2 (10.5 oz.) cans cream of chicken soup
2 C. half-and-half

1 (10 oz.) package frozen chopped spinach, thawed and drained
1/2 tsp thyme
1/4 tsp ground black pepper

Directions

1. In a pan of the boiling water, cook the chicken for about 7-10 minutes.
2. Strain the broth into a large soup pan and bring to a boil.
3. Add the cheese tortellini and gently, stir to combine.
4. Reduce the heat to medium-low and simmer for about 8 minutes.
5. Stir in the chicken, cream of chicken soup, half-and-half, spinach, thyme and black pepper and bring to a simmer.
6. Simmer for about 7-10 minutes.
7. Serve hot.

Great Northern
Pesto Chicken Soup

🥣 Prep Time: 10 mins
🕐 Total Time: 40 mins

Servings per Recipe: 8

Calories	203 kcal
Fat	5.9 g
Carbohydrates	25g
Protein	13.4 g
Cholesterol	19 mg
Sodium	241 mg

Ingredients

1 tbsp olive oil
1/2 lb. boneless skinless chicken breasts cut into bite-size pieces
1 onion, finely diced
3 (14.5 oz.) cans chicken broth
1 (14.5 oz.) can whole peeled tomatoes
1 (14 oz.) can great Northern beans, rinsed and drained
2 carrots, sliced

1 large potato, diced
1/4 tsp salt
1/4 tsp ground black pepper
1 C. frozen green beans
1/4 C. pesto

Directions

1. In a large pan, heat the oil on medium-high heat and cook the chicken for about 5 minutes.
2. Add the onion and cook for about 2 minutes.
3. Add the chicken broth, undrained tomatoes, northern beans, carrots, potato, salt and pepper and bring to a boil, stirring to break up the tomatoes.
4. Reduce the heat to low and simmer, covered for about 15 minutes, stirring occasionally.
5. Add the green beans and simmer for about 5 minutes.
6. Transfer the soup in the serving bowls and serve with a topping of the pesto and Parmesan cheese.

ENJOY THE RECIPES?

KEEP ON COOKING
WITH 6 MORE FREE COOKBOOKS!

Visit our website and simply enter your email address to join the club and receive your 6 cookbooks.

http://booksumo.com/magnet

https://www.instagram.com/booksumopress/

https://www.facebook.com/booksumo/

Printed in the USA
CPSIA information can be obtained
at www.ICGtesting.com
LVHW081948261124
797692LV00012B/1069